ON THE HUNT

RABBIT AND SQUIRREL HUNTING

BY ROXANNE TROUP

EPIC

EPIC, AN IMPRINT OF BELLWETHER MEDIA BY FLUTTERBEE

EPIC

EPIC BOOKS are no ordinary books. They burst with intense action, high-speed heroics, and shadows of the unknown. Are you ready for an Epic adventure?

This edition first published in 2027 by Bellwether Media, Inc.

For information regarding permission, write to Bellwether Media, Inc., Attention: Permissions Department, 3500 American Blvd W, Suite 150, Bloomington, MN 55431.

Library of Congress Cataloging-in-Publication Data

Names: Troup, Roxanne author
Title: Rabbit and squirrel hunting / by Roxanne Troup.
Description: Minneapolis, Minnesota : Bellwether Media, Inc, 2027. | Series: On the hunt | Includes bibliographical references and index. | Audience: Ages 8-12 | Audience: Grades 4-6 |
Summary: "Engaging images accompany information about rabbit and squirrel hunting. The combination of high-interest subject matter and light text is intended for students in grades 2 through 7" -- Provided by publisher.
Identifiers: LCCN 2026001536 (print) | LCCN 2026001537 (ebook) | ISBN 9798898800949 (library binding) | ISBN 9798898802189 (ebook)
Subjects: LCSH: Small game hunting--Juvenile literature | Rabbit hunting--Juvenile literature | Squirrel hunting--Juvenile literature | Hunting--Juvenile literature
Classification: LCC SK340 .T76 2027 (print) | LCC SK340 (ebook)
LC record available at https://lccn.loc.gov/2026001536
LC ebook record available at https://lccn.loc.gov/2026001537

Editor: Ashley Kuehl Designer: Jennifer Bowyer

Printed in the United States of America, North Mankato, MN.

TABLE OF CONTENTS

FIRST HUNT

Two hunters wander through a forest. The older one stops. He quiets his young student. Then he points.

A squirrel dashes across a branch. The student takes **aim** and shoots the squirrel.

TEACHING CONSERVATION

rabbit stew

Rabbits and squirrels live throughout North America. Some people hunt these **small game** animals for food.

RABBIT AND SQUIRREL RANGE

Small game season is long. Most states allow hunting from early fall through late winter. Some allow hunting all year. Large **bag limits** are common.

SO CHEWY

Rabbit and squirrel teeth never stop growing! These animals chew plants to keep their teeth from getting too big.

Young people learn to hunt with small game. They read animal **sign**. They practice shooting and gun safety.

Small game hunting teaches hunters about **conservation**. They grow to respect nature.

FAVORITE HUNTING SPOT

HIAWATHA NATIONAL FOREST, MICHIGAN

- Around **1,406** square miles (3,642 square kilometers) of dense forest
- Long hunting season (September to March)

READY TO HUNT

Small game hunters need less gear than other hunters. A small rifle and hunting knife will do.

HUNTING GEAR

In the woods, hunters wear long pants and hiking boots. Backpacks or **hunting vests** store extra supplies or carry game.

Some hunters use dogs to **flush** small game animals. The dogs are trained to **fetch** kills.

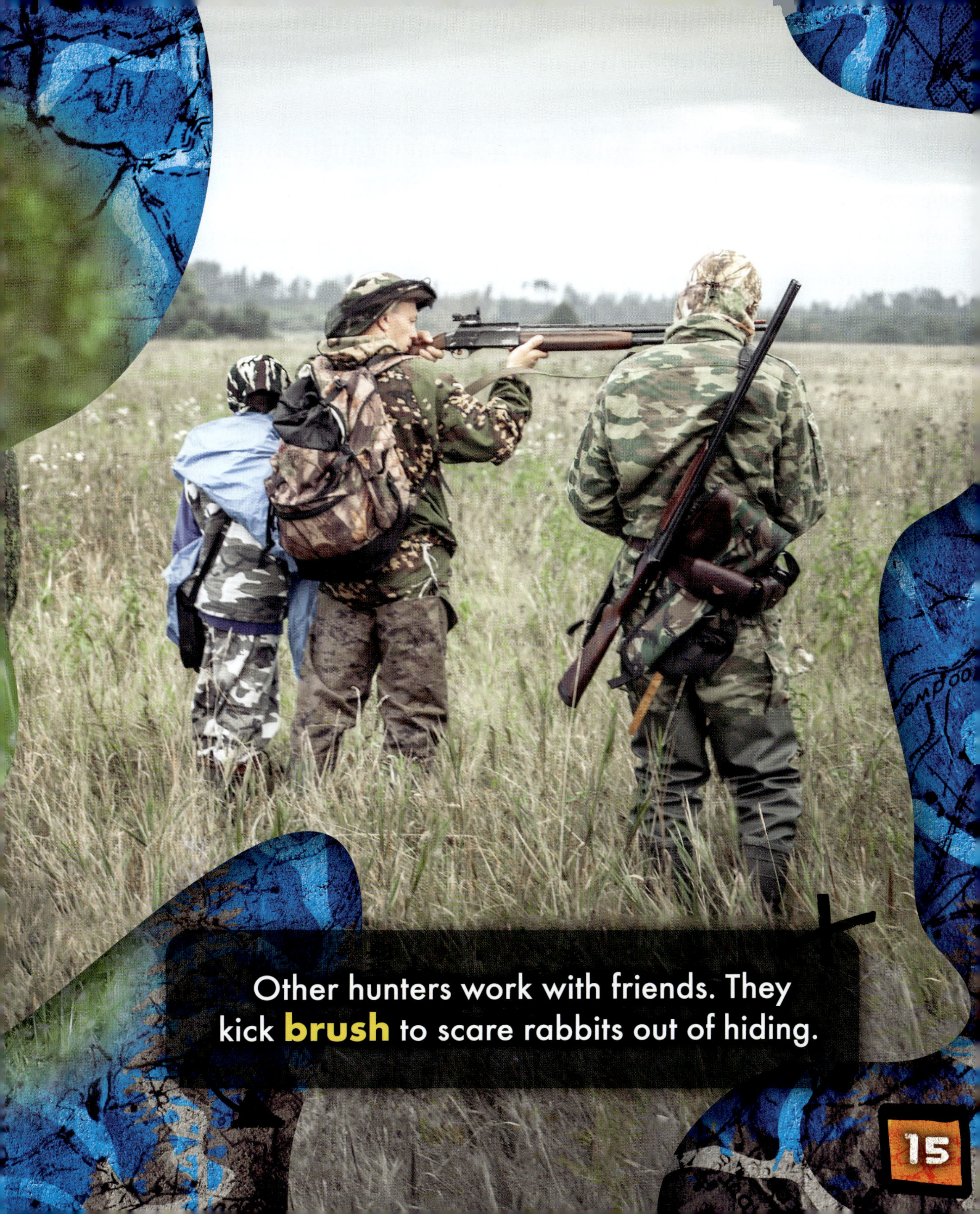

Other hunters work with friends. They kick **brush** to scare rabbits out of hiding.

Some hunters make **snares**. They tie wire in a loop. They set the wire. When an animal comes by, it gets caught in the snare.

AMAZING EARS

Wild rabbits can turn their ears in almost a full circle. That helps them hear danger up to 2 miles (3.2 kilometers) away.

SAFETY FIRST

Few people hunt small game. But its season overlaps other hunting seasons. To stay safe, all hunters should wear **blaze orange**.

Hunters also need a **license**. Paying for a license helps pay for conservation.

STOP, THIEF!

Squirrels lose most of their stored seeds and nuts. Some of this food is stolen by other animals. The rest grows into new plants.

Young hunters should always partner with skilled hunters. Skilled hunters teach gun safety and outdoor skills. They give first aid. They help keep young hunters safe.

GLOSSARY

aim—to point a gun at a target

bag limits—the number of animals one person is allowed to hunt per day

blaze orange—a bright orange color that hunters wear for safety

brush—woody plants and tall weeds

conservation—taking care of the environment

fetch—to bring back

flush—scare an animal out of hiding

hunting vests—sleeveless jackets with big pockets

license—a document that gives hunters legal permission to harvest a certain type of animal

sign—the tracks, markings, and other clues that animals leave in the woods

small game—birds and small animals including rabbits, squirrels, hares, and raccoons

snares—wire loops that tighten around animals' legs or necks to control their movements

TO LEARN MORE

AT THE LIBRARY

Bailey, Diane. *Small Game Hunting.* Minneapolis, Minn.: Lerner Publications, 2024.

Troup, Roxanne. *Pheasant Hunting.* Minneapolis, Minn.: Bellwether Media, 2025.

Wowak, Dan. *Bushcraft Kid: Survive in the Wild and Have Fun Doing It.* Indianapolis, Ind.: DK Kids, 2022.

ON THE WEB

FACTSURFER

Factsurfer.com gives you a safe, fun way to find more information.

1. Go to www.factsurfer.com.
2. Enter "rabbit and squirrel hunting" into the search box and click 🔍.
3. Select your book cover to see a list of related content.

INDEX

The images in this book are reproduced through the courtesy of: Rabbitti, front cover, p. 1; chris froome, front cover, p. 1; Michal, front cover, p. 1; kaninstudio, front cover, p. 1; Kitthanes, p. 3 (rabbit); NafiCraft, p. 3 (squirrel); Nikolay Gyngazov, p. 4; Vicki Beaver/ Alamy Stock Photo, p. 5; brytta, p. 6; StockphotoVideo, p. 6 (stew); Andrew_Howe, p. 7 (profile); IrinaK, p. 7 (profile); MargJohnsonVA, p. 7; 977_ReX_977, p. 8; Robert Winkler, p. 9; EyeEm Mobile GmbH, p. 9 (inset); visualspace, p. 11; Roman Kosolapov, pp. 11 (inset), 21; Myron Muza, p. 12; SolidMaks, p. 13 (rifle, knife); Mountains Hunter, pp. 13 (backpack), 14 (inset); Dainis Zvingulis, p. 13 (pants); Cherkas, p. 13 (boots); PHOVOIR/ Alamy Stock Photo, p. 13; DieterMeyrl, p. 14; splendens, p. 15; Megan Frost Photography, p. 16; Gfed, p. 17; Cavan Images/ Alamy Stock Photo, p. 18; scene_sniper, p. 19; Tetra Images/ Alamy Stock Photo, p. 20; clarst5, p. 23.